First Published by Evans Brothers Limited
2A Portman Mansions,Chiltern Street, London W1U 6NR,
United Kingdom

This edition published under license from Evans Brothers
Limited

North America edition published by Chelsea Clubhouse,
a division of Chelsea House Publishers and a subsidiary of
Haights Cross Communications
2080 Cabot Boulevard West, Suite 201, Langhorne,
PA 19047-1813

Printed in China

Library of Congress Cataloging-in-Publication Data
applied for.

ISBN 0-7910-8180-X

Acknowledgments

The author and publishers would like to thank the following
for their help with this book:

Sam, Kathryn, and Therese Lawton and Hannah and Kate
Clayton.

The publishers would also like to thank The Association of
Wheelchair Children for their help in the preparation of this
book.

All photographs by Gareth Boden

Credits

Series Editor: Louise John
Editor: Julia Bird
Designer: Mark Holt
Production: Jenny Mulvanny

LIKE ME LIKE YOU

Sam Uses a WHEELCHAIR

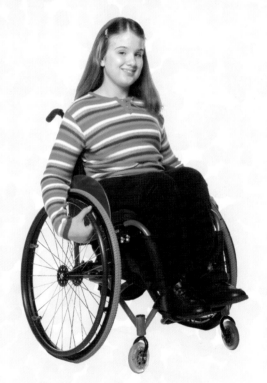

JILLIAN POWELL

CHELSEA CLUBHOUSE
An Imprint of Chelsea House Publishers
A Haights Cross Communications Company
Philadelphia

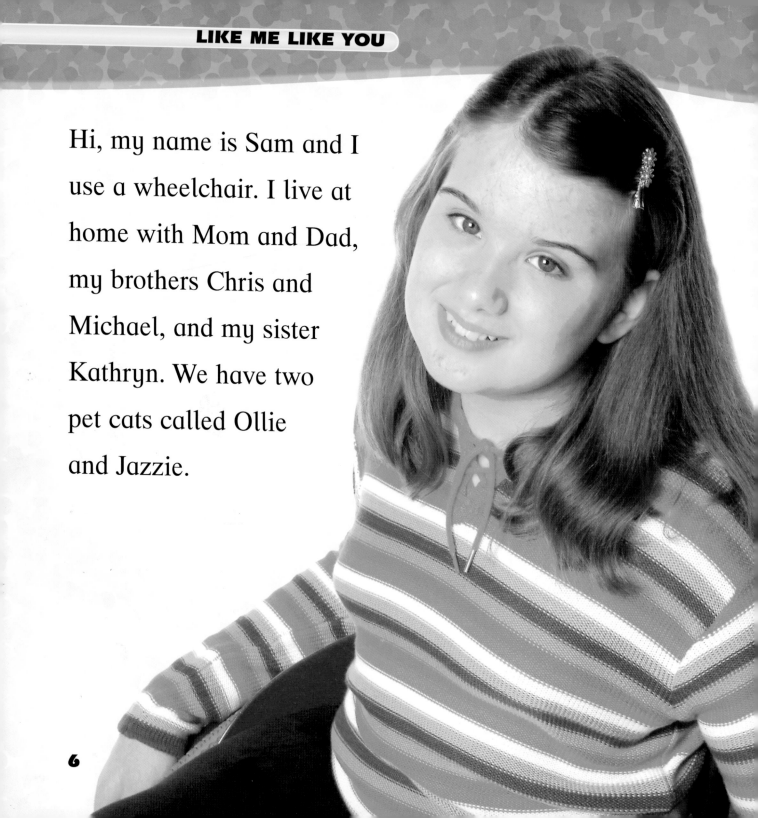

Hi, my name is Sam and I use a wheelchair. I live at home with Mom and Dad, my brothers Chris and Michael, and my sister Kathryn. We have two pet cats called Ollie and Jazzie.

I have **spina bifida**. It means I don't feel anything below my waist, so I have to be careful not to knock or hurt myself. I can't stand or walk easily so I use a wheelchair to get around. This is the chair I use for school and for days out.

SPINA BIFIDA

A baby born with spina bifida has a backbone that doesn't join up properly.

7

I share a bedroom with my sister. We get along well with each other. Sometimes Kathryn gets into one of my wheelchairs and we play games, pushing ourselves around and chasing each other.

I have my own bathroom that's easy for me to use. I can push my chair under the sink to wash my face and brush my teeth. I use a special shower chair when I want to have a shower.

In the morning, I have to do some stretching exercises. I do these twice a day and sometimes in gym at school, too. Mom helps me by gently stretching my legs and feet. This helps them to grow straight.

Then I put on my **splints**. I wear them all day, except when I'm doing sports. They help to keep my legs and feet in place. I like wearing splints in bright colors! I have to wear special shoes with them, but they're nice shoes so I don't mind too much.

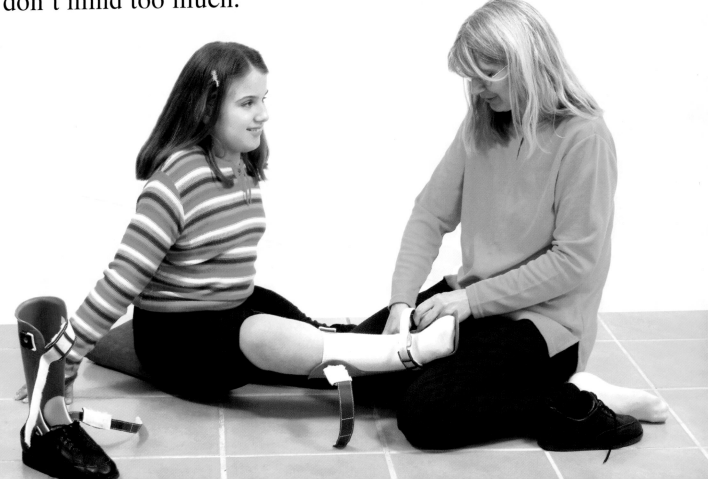

I use this elevator when I want to go downstairs. It goes straight from our bedroom to the kitchen. I like reading there and sometimes I'm so busy reading, I forget to go out!

Today, my friend Hannah has come over to spend the day with me. She likes having a ride in the elevator, too.

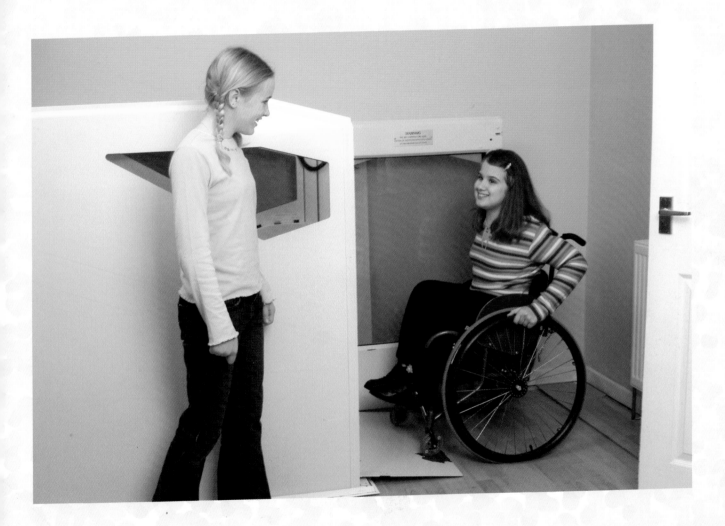

Hannah's coming to the park to watch me practice my wheelchair racing. I go racing every two weeks. It's one of my favorite sports. I wheel myself down the **ramp** outside our house. Ramps make it much easier for me to get around.

Hannah helps Mom get my wheelchair into the car. I have a special wheelchair for racing. It's very light and fast and it has three wheels. I wear a racing helmet and gloves too.

It's great fun wheelchair racing, and it helps keep my arms strong. I try to practice every week. Hannah has a stopwatch so she can time me. I try to go a bit faster each time. Hannah tells me I'm three seconds faster than last time!

Sometimes I enter competitions where I race against other girls and boys in wheelchairs. I show Hannah the medals I've won for winning in three different races.

After the park, Mom takes me and Hannah to a youth club where we do arts and crafts and sometimes sports. We always have a great time and it's a good place to make new friends.

Sometimes we do baking at the club, too. Today, Hannah and I are making cheese pizzas. I'm putting lots of cheese on mine!

There's a special bathroom at the club that's easy for me to use. It has a wide doorway so I can wheel my chair through easily. There are rails for me to hold to lift myself on and off the toilet.

Later, we play a game of table tennis with some friends. The table has high sides that stop the ball from falling on to the floor so I don't have to keep picking it up!

We can do lots of other sports at the club. I like playing basketball. The basket is set low on the wall so that I can reach it more easily.

Sometimes we play a computer dance game. The screen shows you where to put your feet on the dance mats. Hannah has to be quick with her feet! I can follow the dance on the PlayStation. I have to be quick with my fingers!

Being a wheelchair user means I can't do some things as easily as most people, like going over to my friends' houses to play. I spend more time at home, but I love reading, especially adventure books!

There are lots of sports I can do that are fun too, like basketball. I can join in and play with my friends.

Some people need to use wheelchairs because they are born with a disability, like spina bifida or **cerebral palsy**. Others need to use a wheelchair after they have had an accident or illness.

Glossary

Cerebral palsy a condition in which the part of the brain that controls movement is damaged

Ramp a slope in place of steps

Spina bifida a condition in which a baby's backbone does not join up properly before it is born

Splint a hard case that supports and protects parts of the body

Index

Further Information

Winners on Wheels USA (WOW)
800-969-8255

www.wowusa.com

Information and resources to help children in wheelchairs gain life skills and develop creativity. WOW empowers kids in wheelchairs by encouraging personal achievement through creative learning and expanded life experiences. The website includes the following sections: Parent Section, Volunteer Section, Publication Section, and Corporate Section.

WheelchairNet.org
412-383-6793

www.wheelchairnet.org

Information on mobility devices for children and adults. WheelchairNet is a community for people who have a common interest in (or in some cases a passion for) wheelchair technology and its improvement and successful application. Resources include a bibliographic database, a series of slide lectures, article reprints, and an active discussion area. WheelchairNet's purpose is to serve the information needs of anyone interested in wheeled mobility.

Wheelchair Foundation
877-378-3839

www.wheelchairfoundation.org

A nonprofit organization leading an international effort to create awareness of the needs and abilities of people with physical disabilities, to promote the joy of giving, create global friendship, and to deliver a wheelchair to every child, teen, and adult in the world who needs one, but cannot afford one.

BOOKS
Rolling Along: The Story of Taylor and His Wheelchair, Jamee Riggio Heelan et al., Peachtree Publishers, Limited, 2000

Being in a Wheelchair, Lois Keith, Smart Apple Media, 1999

The Berenstain Bears and the Wheelchair Commando, Stan Berenstain et al., Random House Children's Books, 1993

Our Teacher's in a Wheelchair, Mary E. Powers, Albert Whitman & Company, 1986

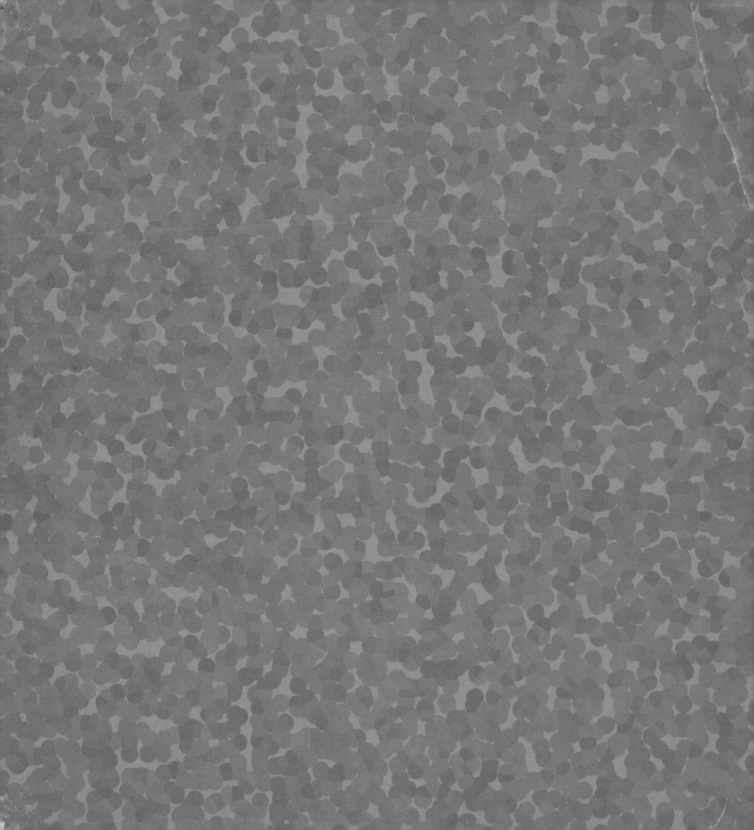